Southeast Asia

Make the most of your time on Earth

ROUGH GUIDES

25 YEARS 1982–2007

NEW YORK • LONDON • DELHI

Contents

Introduction 4–5

01 Exploring the temples of Angkor 8–9 **02 Partying** at the Ati-Atihan festival 10–11 **03 Taking** the slow boat down the Mekong 12–13 **04 Budget** beach-chic in Thailand 14–15 **05 Karst and crew**: staying overnight on Ha Long Bay 16–17 **06 Saffron and gold**: falling under the spell of Louang Phabang 18–19 **07 A night** in the rainforest, Taman Negara 20–21 **08 Climbing** the stairway to heaven in Banaue 22–23 **09 Moonlit** meanders through Hoi An 24–25 **10 Diving** the Tubbataha Reef 26–27 **11 Acquiring** the taste: cookery lessons in Thailand 28–29 **12 Conquering** Southeast Asia's highest peak: Mount Kinabalu 30–31 **13 Meeting** the relatives: Orang-utan encounters in Sumatra 32–33 **14 Paddling** into secret lagoons, Phang Nga 34–35 **15 Joining** the party at an Iban longhouse 36–37 **16 Ironing** out the kinks in Thailand 38–39 **17 The biggest** buddhist stupa in the world: Borobudur 40–41 **18 Shopping** for Thailand at Chatuchak Weekend Market 42–43 **19 Braving** the dragons' den on Komodo Island 44–45 **20 The hills** are alive: trekking in northern Thailand 46–47 **21 Island-hopping** in the Bacuit archipelago 48–49 **22 Balinese theatrics** in Indonesia 50–51 **23 Visiting** the Tuol Sleng Genocide Museum 52–53 **24 Volcanic activity**: sunrise on Mount Bromo 54–55 **25 Feeling** fruity in the Mekong Delta 56–57

Miscellany 59–72

Small print & Rough Guides info 73–79

Index 80

Introduction

EXPERIENCES have always been at the heart of the Rough Guide concept. A group of us began writing the books **25 years ago** (hence this celebratory mini series) and wanted to share the kind of travels we had been doing ourselves. It seems bizarre to recall that in the early 1980s, travel was very much a minority pursuit. Sure, there was a lot of tourism around, and that was reflected in the guidebooks in print, which traipsed around the established sights with scarcely a backward look at the local population and their life. We wanted to change all that: to put a country or a city's popular culture centre stage, to highlight the clubs where you could hear local music, drink with people you hadn't come on holiday with, watch the local football, join in with the festivals. And of course we wanted to push travel a bit further, inspire readers with the confidence and knowledge to break away from established routes, to find pleasure and excitement in remote islands, or desert routes, or mountain treks, or in street culture.

Twenty-five years on, that thinking seems pretty obvious: we all want to experience something real about a destination, and to seek out travel's **ultimate experiences**. Which is exactly where these **25 books** come in. They are not in any sense a new series of guidebooks. We're happy with the series that we already have in print. Instead, the **25s** are a collection of ideas, enthusiasms and inspirations: a selection of the very best things to see or do – and not just before you die, but now. Each selection is gold dust. That's the brief to our writers: there is no room here for the average, no space fillers. Pick any one of our selections and you will enrich your travelling life.

But first of all, take the time to browse. Grab a half dozen of these books and let the ideas percolate … and then begin making your plans.

Mark Ellingham
Founder & Series Editor, Rough Guides

25

Ultimate
experiences
Southeast
Asia

1

Exploring the temples of Angkor, Cambodia

Every tour of Cambodia's Angkorian ruins begins with **Angkor Wat**, an awesomely grand design of encircling colonnades, elegant stepped towers and an astonishing gallery of bas-reliefs. It's the largest and most famous of the countless state temples built by the Hindu–Buddhist Khmers, whose vast empire extended west to Burma and south into Malaysia and lasted from the ninth to the fifteenth centuries. Successive kings made their mark, leaving the Angkor region – their heartland – filled with hundreds of impressive relics. The beautifully proportioned

Give yourself at least three days for exploring the temples, so you have time to see half a dozen of the best and can also return to your favourites, preferably at a different time of day – noontime is refreshingly quiet as tour groups return to town for lunch. The temples are open daily 5.30am–6.30pm; 1/4/7-day passes cost $20/40/60. The main site entrance is 5km from Siem Reap, which is served by flights from Phnom Penh and Bangkok and by bus and boat from Phnom Penh. Transport between temples is by bicycle, motorbike taxi, tuk tuk or car.

Angkor Wat, with its iconic west elevation, is undoubtedly the most magnificent, but you'd be missing many spectacular sights if you stopped your tour there.

After Angkor Wat, top of the list is the walled royal city of **Angkor Thom**, whose southern causeway is guarded by rows of dignified stone sentries: almond-eyed gods on the left, round-eyed demons to the right. Beyond them, its claustrophobic inner sanctum, the Bayon, is crowded with scores of colossal Buddha-like heads, carved from massive stone blocks atop disorienting, looming towers. **Ta Prohm** is next, its

porticos conjuring images of a tomb-raiding Lara Croft. Head-high buttress roots clamp balustraded windows, lianas tangle and probe, and you're reminded that until the late nineteenth century every one of Angkor's temples was enveloped like this. On to **Banteay Srei**, ten kilometres away, whose pink sandstone facades are covered in exquisite depictions of life and ritual in tenth-century Cambodia. And finally head up to remote, hillside **Kbal Spean**, where even the riverbed has been carved with Hindu gods so that the water is continually sanctified as it washes down into

2 Partying at the Ati-Atihan festival, the Philippines

You need serious stamina for the three days and nights of non-stop dancing that mark the culmination of **Ati-Atihan**, the most flamboyant fiesta in the **fiesta-mad Philippines**. No wonder the mantra chanted by participants in this marathon rave is *hala bira, puera pasma*, which means **"keep on going, no tiring"**. If you plan on lasting the course, start training now.

Ati-Atihan, which takes place during the first two weeks of January in Kalibo – an otherwise unimpressive port town on the central Philippine island of Panay – actually lasts for two weeks. But it's the final three days that are the most important, with costumed locals taking to the streets in **a riot of spontaneous partying, music and street dancing**. And it's this the tourists come for – **72 sleepless hours** of alcohol-fuelled, intoxicating mayhem acted out to the deafening ranks of massed tribal drums.

Don't expect to just stand by and watch – the locals have an unwritten rule that there are no wallflowers at Ati-Atihan – and **if you don't take part, they'll make you**. Even if all you can muster is a drunken conga line, you can take the edge off your nerves with a few glasses of *lambanog*, a vigorous native aperitif made from leftover jackfruit or mango fermented in cheap containers buried in the earth – the **"zombie flavour"** is especially liberating.

Ati-Atihan is still partly a religious festival, held to celebrate the child Jesus (Santo Niño). In recent years it has morphed into **a delightful hodge-podge of Catholic ritual, indigenous drama and tourist attraction**. It's the one time of the year when Catholic Filipinos aren't afraid to push the boat out, especially for the **final-day fancy dress parade** that sees thousands of people in costumes so big and brash they almost block the street.

If you're feeling a little rough after all this, do what many others do and head up the coast to the beautiful little island of Boracay, where you can **sleep off your hangover on one of the finest beaches in the world**.

need to know

Kalibo is a one-hour flight south of the Philippine capital, Manila. Hotels are usually full for Ati-Atihan, so book well in advance.

Cargo-hold hell used to be the order of the day for travellers taking the slow boat through Laos, squashed between chickens and sacks of rice. But the ride's become so popular that there are now **specially designed backpackers' boats** running the 300-kilometre route from the Thai border east to Louang Phabang. They even have proper seats and a toilet – both pretty handy when you're spending two long days on the river. It's still a **cramped, bottom-numbing experience** though, with over a hundred passengers on board, and an average speed that's very slow indeed.

In truth you wouldn't expect a trip on **Southeast Asia's longest and most important river** to be plain sailing. Here in northern Laos, approximately halfway down the river's **4000-kilometre journey** from its source on the Tibetan plateau to its delta in southern Vietnam, the Mekong is dogged by sandbanks and seasonal shallows. It can be tough to navigate, as passengers in the hurtling, accident-prone speedboats often discover. Better to **take it slowly**; bring a cushion and enjoy the ride.

Little about the river has changed over the decades. **The Mekong has always been a lifeline for Laos**, Southeast Asia's only landlocked nation, and villagers continue to depend on it for fish, irrigation and transport, even **panning its silt in search of gold**. Limestone cliffs and thickly forested hills frame its banks, with riverside clearings used for **banana groves**, **slash-and-burn agriculture** and **bamboo-shack villages**. The largest of these, Pakbeng, marks the journey's mid-point, where everyone disembarks for a night on dry land. A ramshackle place for such an important river port, Pakbeng offers an unvarnished introduction to Laos, with rudimentary guest houses and just four hours of electricity a day. Roll on the civilized comforts of Louang Phabang, a mere eight hours downriver.

need to know

Slow boats leave when full and run from Houayxai on the Thai–Lao border to Louang Phabang ($18) and vice versa; take food and

Taking the
slow boat
down the
Mekong

3

O ld-school travellers complain that Thailand has gone upmarket, swapped its cheap sleeps for identikit villas and sacrificed the beach-shack-and-hammock vibe for apartments with swimming pools. They've got a point. Thailand is prospering: new boutique hotels entice you with minimalist curves and luxurious fabrics, and at $150 a night, a five-star suite can seem like an affordable indulgence.

But the rudimentary bamboo beach huts still exist and arguably there's no better way to experience the pleasures of Thailand's gorgeous strands. With over 3000 kilometres of coastline and scores of accessible islands you've got plenty of beaches to choose from, the default option being squeaky white sand and luminous turquoise water. Staying in a wooden hut you're often all but camping: you'll see the sand beneath your feet through the slats of the wonky planked floor; you'll hear the waves lapping the shoreline just a few metres from your

4

Budget
beach-chic
in Thailand

ill-fitting front door; and there's no need for a fan when you prop open the woven rattan shutters and let the breeze waft through. Make your own shell mobiles, hang your sarong as a door curtain and string up your hammock. It's your very own eco home and worth every bit of the modest daily sum that buys you residency.

need to know

The simplest beach huts share bathrooms, have electricity for only a few hours each night and cost about $4 per night for two people sharing. Among Thailand's best old-style beach huts are: **KP Huts**, which are scattered through a shoreside coconut grove on Ko Chang (☎+66 (0)84 099 5100); the rough-hewn timber huts with stripey doors and matching deckchairs at **Island Hut** on Ko Mak (☎+66 (0)87 139 5537); and **Bee Bee Bungalow**'s idiosyncratic experiments in bamboo architecture on Ko Lanta (☎+66 (0)81 537 9932, @www.diigii.de).

5

Karst and crew: staying overnight on Ha Long Bay, Vietnam

S pend a night afloat among the limestone pinnacles of Ha Long Bay, and you'll witness their many moods as their silhouettes morph with the moonlight, mist and midday sun. Scores of local boat companies offer this experience, for the spectacularly scenic bay is a World Heritage site and Vietnam's top tourist destination.

Regularly referred to as the eighth natural wonder of the world, the 1500 square kilometres of Ha Long Bay contain nearly two thousand islands, most uninhabited outcrops that protrude evocatively from the Gulf of Tonkin. Their intriguingly craggy profiles have long inspired poets, wags and travel writers to wax lyrical about Italianate cathedrals, every type of creature from fighting cock to bug-eyed frog, even famous faces, but the bay's creation myth is just as poetic. "*Ha Long*" translates as "the dragon descending into the sea", for legend tells how the islets were scattered here by the celestial dragon as a barrier against invaders.

Even the most imaginative visitor might tire of interpreting the shapes for a full two days, so overnight trips offer different angles on rock appreciation. As well as lounging on island beaches by day and swimming the phosphorescent waters by night, there are plenty of caves and floating villages to explore, and endless fresh seafood to enjoy. Some tours allow you to paddle yourself around in a kayak, while others feature forest treks and cycle rides on Cat Ba Island, the largest in the bay.

need to know

Most people arrange all-inclusive tours of the bay from Hanoi, about 150km away. These cost from $40 for three-day budget trips (ⓦwww. vietnamsunshinetravel.com) to $100 for two-day luxury cruises (ⓦwww. handspan.com). The cheapest tours run out of Cat Ba Island (**Family Hotel Quang Duc**; ☎+84(0)31/888231; from $10 per person per day). The best time to visit the bay is from April to October; February and March can be chilly and drizzly.

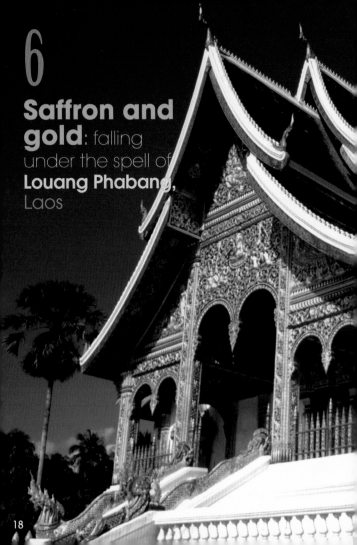

6
Saffron and gold: falling under the spell of **Louang Phabang,** Laos

The pace of life is deliciously slow in Louang Phabang, but if you opt for a lie-in you'll miss the perfect start to the day. As dawn breaks over this most languorous of Buddhist towns, saffron-robed monks emerge from their temple-monasteries to collect alms from their neighbours, the riverbanks begin to hum and the smell of freshly baked baguettes draws you to one of the many cafés. It's a captivating scene whichever way you turn: ringed by mountains and encircled by the Mekong and Khan rivers, the old quarter's temple roofs peep out from the palm groves, its streets still lined with wood-shuttered shophouses and French-colonial mansions.

Though it has the air of a rather grand village, Louang Phabang is the ancient Lao capital, seat of the royal family that ruled the country for six hundred years until the Communists exiled them in the 1970s. It remains the most cultured town in Laos (not a hard-won accolade it's true, in this poor, undeveloped nation), and one of the best preserved in Southeast Asia – now formalized by its World Heritage status. Chief among its many beautiful temples is the entrancing sixteenth-century Wat Xiang Thong, whose tiered roofs frame an exquisite glass mosaic of the tree of life and attendant creatures, flanked by pillars and doors picked out in brilliant gold-leaf stencils. It's a gentle stroll from here to the graceful teak and rosewood buildings of the Royal Palace Museum and the dazzling gilded murals of neighbouring Wat Mai.

When you tire of the monuments, there are riverside caves, waterfalls and even a whisky-making village to explore, and plenty of shops selling intricate textiles and Hmong hill-tribe jewellery. Serenity returns at sunset, when the monks' chants drift over the temple walls and everyone else heads for high ground to soak up the view.

need to know

Louang Phabang is served by flights from the Thai cities of Bangkok and Chiang Mai and from the Lao capital, Vientiane. It can also be reached by bus and boat from Vientiane and by boat from the Thai–Lao border at Chiang Khong/Houayxai.

You probably won't get much sleep on your first night in Taman Negara national park – not because there's an elephant honking on your chalet doorstep or the rain's dripping through your tent, but because the rainforest is unexpectedly noisy after dark. High-volume insects whirr and beep at an ear-splitting pitch, branches creak and swish menacingly, and every so often something nearby shrieks or thumps. Taman Negara is a deceptively busy place, home to scores of different creatures including commonly sighted *macaques*, *gibbons*, *leaf monkeys* and *tapir*, as well as more elusive *tigers*, *elephants* and *sun bears*. Not to mention some three hundred species of birds and an inordinate insect population.

Many rainforest residents are best observed after dark, either on a *ranger-led night walk* or from one of the twelve-bed tree-house hides strategically positioned above popular

A NIGHT IN THE RAINFOREST

TAMAN NEGARA, MALAYSIA

salt licks. But a longer guided trek also offers a good chance of spotting something interesting and will get you immersed in the phenomenally diverse flora of Taman Negara, which supports a staggering 14,000 plant species, including 75-metre-high *tualang trees*, carnivorous *pitcher plants* and fungi that glow like lightbulbs. The rewarding six-hour *Keniam–Trenggan trail* takes you through dense jungle and into several impressive caves, while the arduous week-long expedition to the cloudforests atop 2187-metre-high *Gunung Tahan* involves frequent river crossings and steep climbs. With minimal effort, on the other hand, you can ascend to the treetops near park headquarters, via a canopy walkway. Slung thirty metres above the forest floor between a line of towering *tualang* trees, this swaying bridge offers a gibbon's perspective on the cacophonous jungle below.

need to know

Taman Negara (🌐www.wildlife.gov.my; entry $4) is 250km from Kuala Lumpur and can be reached by bus or, more enjoyably, by train and boat. There's accommodation to suit all budgets in the village of Kuala Tahan, at Taman Negara headquarters, and elsewhere within the park. The canopy walkway is open every day from 9am to 3pm (until noon on Fridays) and costs $1.25. A guided trek up Gunung Tahan must be booked a month in advance and costs $125 per group of up to twelve.

8

Climbing the stairway to heaven

Lay them
out end-to-end and they'd
stretch from Scandinavia to the South Pole.
No wonder the tribes of Ifugao province, in the beautiful northern
Philippines, call the Banaue rice terraces their stairways to heaven.

The terraces are one of this country's great icons, hewn from the
land two thousand years ago by tribespeople using primitive tools,
an achievement that ranks alongside the building of the pyramids.
They are a truly awesome sight. Cut into near-vertical slopes, the
water-filled ledges curve around the hills' winding contours, their
waters reflecting the pale green of freshly planted rice stalks. And
unlike other old wonders of engineering, the terraces are still in the
making after two millennia. Employing spades and digging sticks,
countless generations of Ifugao farmers have cultivated rice on
thousands of these mountainside paddies. Constantly guarding
them against natural erosion, they have fortified the terraces with
packed-earth and loose-stone retaining walls, supporting an
elaborate system of dykes.

in Banaue, the Philippines

A few kilometres up the road from Banaue town is a popular lookout point that offers a sweeping vista down a wide valley with terraces on both sides. It's a great view, but it's not the only one. To really get to know the landscape the only way is on foot. Dozens of narrow paths snake their way past thundering waterfalls into a dazzling green hinterland of monolithic steps. If you're looking for rural isolation and unforgettable rice-terrace scenery, the fifteen-kilometre trek from Banaue to the remote little tribal village of Batad simply shouldn't be missed. Batad nestles in a natural amphitheatre, close to the glorious Tappia Tappia Waterfall. Accommodation here is basic, but it doesn't matter. In the semi-dark, after a long trek and a swim in the falls, you can sit on your verandah, listening to the hiss of cicadas and the squawk of giant bats, transfixed by the looming silhouettes of the surrounding mountains.

23

Moonlit meanders

9

through Hoi An, Vietnam

Once a month, on the eve of the full moon, Hoi An turns off all its street lights and basks in the mellow glow of silk lanterns. Shopkeepers don traditional outfits; parades, folk opera and martial arts demonstrations flood the cobbled streets; and the riverside fills with stalls selling crabmeat parcels, beanpaste cakes and noodle soup. It's all done for tourists of course – and some find it cloyingly self-conscious – but nevertheless this historic little central Vietnam town oozes charm, with the monthly Full Moon Festival just part of its appeal.

Much of the town's charisma derives from its downtown architecture. Until the Thu Bon River silted up in the late eighteenth century, Hoi An was an important port, attracting traders from China and beyond, many of whom settled and built wooden-fronted homes, ornate shrines and exuberantly tiled Assembly Halls that are still used by their descendants today. Several of these atmospheric buildings are now open to the public, offering intriguing glimpses into cool, dark interiors filled with imposing furniture, lavishly decorated altars and family memorabilia that have barely been touched since the 1800s. Together with the peeling pastel facades, colonnaded balconies and waterside market, it's all such a well-preserved blast from the past that UNESCO has designated central Hoi An a World Heritage site.

The merchant spirit needs no such protection, however: there are now so many shops in this small town that the authorities have recently imposed a ban on any new openings. Art galleries and antique shops are plentiful, but silk and tailoring are the biggest draws. Hoi An tailors are the best in the country, and for $200 you can walk away with an entire custom-made wardrobe – complete with Armani-inspired suit, silk shirt, hand-crafted leather boots and personalized handbag. And if you've really fallen under Hoi An's spell, you might find yourself also ordering an *ao dai*, the tunic and trouser combo worn so elegantly by Vietnamese women.

need to know

Hoi An is around 700km south of Hanoi. The nearest airport and train station are in Da Nang, a thirty-kilometre taxi ride away. Welcoming little *Thien Tanh Hotel* (Ⓦwww.bluesky-hoian.com; doubles from $20) is set beside ricefields and makes a lovely place to stay.

If you're looking for some of the most adventurous and thrilling scuba diving in the world, never mind Southeast Asia, **Tubbataha Reef Marine Park** in the Sulu Sea is the place to start. Well out of sight of land and almost two hundred kilometres southeast of Puerto Princesa in Palawan, this World Heritage site is only accessible on **live-aboard boats** when seas are favourable, between March and June. But its very isolation means it's **not overrun by package-tour divers**, and even during these peak months you'll probably be on one of only a handful of small boats in the area. The reef – actually a grouping of dozens of small reefs, atolls and coral islands **covering more than 300 square kilometres** – is one of the finest in the world, with daily sightings of the big pelagics that all divers dream of.

Rise at dawn for a quick **dive among the turtles and small sharks** before breakfast. Afterwards there's time for a visit to **Shark Airport**, where sharks "take off" from sandy ledges like planes, before it's back to the boat for lunch and a snooze. You can do **deep dives**, **night dives**, **drift dives**, **all kinds of dives**. Or you can simply fossick gently along some of the shallower reefs, home to so many varieties of coral and fish that it's hard to know where to look next. For a real buzz, dive deep over one of the many **coral walls that seem to plunge into infinity** and hang out for a few minutes with **giant manta rays**, **black-tip reef sharks** and, just possibly, cruising **hammerheads**. You also stand a good chance of getting up close and personal with a whale shark, the harmless gentle giants of the sea known in the Philippines as *butanding*.

Of course, there's **life beyond diving at Tubbataha**. For a change of scene, you can snorkel around some of the atolls, **picnic on the beach** at the ranger station, or just kick back on deck and **watch dolphins and tuna perform** occasional aerial stunts.

need to know

Philippines-based dive operators such as **Scuba World** (@www.scubaworld.com.ph), **Dive Buddies** (@www.divephil.com) and **Asia Divers** (@www.asiadivers.com) organize trips out of Puerto Princesa, which is less than two hours from Manila by plane. Packages cost around $1200–1400 for a one-week trip, including domestic flights, food and

10 Diving the Tubbataha Reef

Half the fun of foreign travel is trying new food – roast duck curry, sticky rice with mango, even deep-fried locusts. So what better souvenir to return home with than the knowledge of how to recreate the tastiest dishes yourself?

Thailand offers scores of different cookery classes for tourists, held in restaurants, hotels and guest houses all over the country. Lessons begin at

need to know: One-day courses cost from $26 to $120. Recommended schools include the residential **Thai House** outside Bangkok (ⓦwww.thaihouse.co.th); **May Kaidee** vegetarian restaurant in Bangkok (ⓦwww.maykaidee.com); and the **Chiang Mai Thai Cookery School** in Chiang Mai (ⓦwww.thaicookeryschool.com).

the market, where your teacher guides you through the piles of roots and little green leaves so crucial to Thai cuisine. Basil, lemon grass, galangal and chilli are major players, usually combined with coconut milk, lime juice or fermented fish sauce. Back at the wok, you're shown how to work these up into an authentic Thai meal, which should feature just the right balance of salty, sour, spicy and sweet flavours. And you realize how little time it takes to flash-fry beef in oyster sauce or throw together a coconut chicken soup – one of the reasons it's safe to eat at almost any hot-food street stall in Thailand where the dish is cooked right there in front of you.

Thais snack throughout the day, scoffing slices of pomelo fruit dipped in a sugar, salt and chilli mix as a mid-morning refresher, a stick of chicken satay on the way home from work. In the evening it's usual to eat at the night market. With as many as fifty different stalls to choose from, these

11 Acquiring the taste:
cookery lessons in Thailand

are great places to broaden your culinary horizons and at a dollar a dish you can afford to experiment. After a gourmet session, you'll be bursting to add some new recipes to your repertoire, including: the famous hot and sour prawn soup, *tom yam kung*; the classic chicken with cashew nuts; and perhaps the mouth-blasting *som tam*, green papaya and chilli salad, if only to show what an authentically Thai palate you've acquired.

t's a hell of a slog up Malaysian Borneo's Mount Kinabalu, but every year thousands of visitors brave the freezing conditions and risk of altitude sickness to reach the 4095-metre-high summit. The reward is a spectacular dawn panorama across granite pinnacles rising out of the clouds below you – and the knowledge that you've conquered the highest peak between the Himalayas and New Guinea.

Your two-day expedition up the southern ridge begins at Kinabalu Park headquarters, where you meet your obligatory guide and gulp at the multiple jagged peaks ahead. You need to be equipped as for any mountain hike, prepared for downpours and extreme chill at the summit, but Kinabalu's appeal is that any averagely fit tourist can reach the top. The steady climb up to the Laban Rata mountain huts is a five-hour trek along a well-tramped trail through changing forest habitats. Beyond 1800m you're in dense cloudforest, among a thousand species of orchids, 26 types of rhododendron and a host of insect-hungry pitcher plants. By 2600m most of the vegetation has given up, but you stagger on to 3300m and the long-awaited flop into bed. Day two starts at 2.30am for the final push across the glistening granite rock face to Low's Peak, Kinabalu's highest point. It's dark and very cold; for three hours you see no further than the beam of your headtorch and, despite the handrails and ropes, the climb is tough; some have to turn back because of pounding altitude headaches. But when you finally reach the summit, your spirit rises with the sun as the awesome view comes into focus, your every horizon filled with the stark grey twists of Kinabalu's iconic peaks, the mile-deep chasm of infamous Low's Gully at your feet.

need to know

Kinabalu Park headquarters (ⓦwww.suterasanctuarylodges.com) issues permits ($27) and organizes guides (from $19 per group) and porters. Accommodation must be reserved ahead and costs from $12 for a dorm bed, both at headquarters and on the mountain. Kinabalu Park is a two-hour bus ride from Kota Kinabalu, the capital of the East Malaysian state of Sabah.

Conquering
Southeast Asia's highest peak:
Mount Kinabalu, Malaysia

Orang-utan encounters in Sumatra

Sandwiched between the raging Bohorok River and the deep, silent, steaming jungle, the Bukit Lawang Orang-utan Sanctuary, on the vast Indonesian island of Sumatra, offers the unique opportunity of witnessing one of our closest and most charming relatives in their own backyard.

Having crossed the Bohorok on a precarious, makeshift canoe, your first sight of these kings of the jungle is at the enclosures housing recent arrivals, many of whom have been rescued from the thriving trade in exotic pets, particularly in nearby Singapore. It's here that the long process of rehabilitation begins, a process that may include learning from their human guardians such basic simian skills as tree-climbing and fruit-peeling.

Most of these activities are done away from the prying cameras of tourists, but twice a day park officers lead visitors up to a feeding platform to wait, and to watch. The sound of rustling foliage and creaking branches betrays the presence of a rangy, shaggy silhouette making its languid yet majestic way through the treetops. Orang-utans literally force the trees to bend to their will as they swing back and forth on one sapling until the next can be reached. Swooping just above the awestruck audience, they arrive at the platform to feast on bananas and milk, the diet kept deliberately monotonous to encourage the orang-utans – all of whom have been recently released from the sanctuary – to look for more diverse flavours in the forest.

Once the ape has proved that it's capable of surviving unaided, it will be left to fend for itself in the vast, dark forests of north Sumatra. Its rehabilitation will be considered complete. Sadly, at Bukit Lawang there never seems to be a shortage of rescued apes to take its place.

need to know

Bukit Lawang is a three-hour bus ride from Medan. The sanctuary is only open to visitors during the twice-daily feeding sessions at 8am and 3pm, for which you need to buy a permit ($2) from the Bohorok Visitor Centre in the village.

Paddling into *secret lagoons*

Phang Nga

The first time you enter a *hong* you're almost certain to laugh with delight.

The fun begins when your guide paddles you across to the towering karst island and then pilots your canoe through an imperceptible fissure in its rock wall. You enter a sea cave that reeks of bats which gets darker and darker until suddenly your guide shouts "Lie back in the boat please!". Your nose barely clears the stalactites and you emerge, toes first, into a sun-lit lagoon, or *hong*, at the heart of the outcrop.

Hong ("rooms" in Thai) are the *pièce de résistance* of southern Thailand's Phang Nga Bay. Invisible to any passing vessel, these secret tidal lagoons are flooded, roofless caves hidden within the core of seemingly solid limestone islands, accessible only at certain tides and only in sea canoes small enough to slip beneath and between low-lying rocky overhangs. Like the islands themselves, the *hong* have taken millions of years to form, with the softer limestone hollowed out from the side by the pounding waves, and from above by the wind and the rain.

The world inside these collapsed cave systems is extraordinary, protected from the open bay by a turreted ring of cliffs hung with primeval-looking gardens of inverted cycads, twisted bonsai palms, lianas, miniature screw pines and tangled ferns. And as the tide withdraws, the *hong*'s resident creatures – among them fiddler crabs, mudskippers, dusky langurs and crab-eating macaques – emerge to forage on the muddy floor, while white-bellied sea eagles hover expectantly overhead.

need to know: Phang Nga Bay covers some 400 square kilometres of coast between Phuket and Krabi and can be explored from either place. The most spectacular *hong* lie within the island of Ko Panak, in the western bay, where limestone cliffs hide tunnels to no fewer than five different tidal lagoons. A reputable operator of sea-canoeing trips around the bay is **John Gray's Sea Canoe** (@www.johngray-seacanoe.com); day-trips cost from $90 per person.

It's always polite to bring gifts to your hosts' house, but when visiting a Sarawak longhouse make sure it's something that's easily shared, as longhouses are communal, and nearly everything gets divvied up into equal parts. This isn't always an easy task: typically, longhouses are home to around 150 people and contain at least thirty family apartments, each one's front door opening on to the common gallery, hence the tag "a thirty-door longhouse" to describe the size. These days not everyone lives there full time, but the majority of Sarawak's indigenous Iban population still consider the longhouse home, even if they only return for weekends.

Many longhouses enjoy stunning locations, usually in a clearing beside a river, so you'll probably travel to yours in a longboat that meanders between the jungle-draped banks, dodging logs being floated downstream to the timber yards. Look carefully and you'll see that patches of hinterland have been cultivated with black pepper vines, rubber and fruit trees, plus the occasional square of paddy, all of which are crucial to longhouse economies.

need to know: The easiest way to arrange a night in a longhouse is via a tour company based in the Sarawak capital, Kuching. **Borneo Transverse** (@www.borneotransverse.com.my) and **Borneo Adventure** (@www.borneoadventure.com) charge from $30 per person per day.

Having firstly met the chief of your longhouse, you climb the notched tree trunk that serves as a staircase into the stilted wooden structure and enter the common area, or *ruai*, a wide gallery that runs the length of the building and is the focus of community social life. Pretty much everything happens here – the meeting and greeting, the giving and sharing of gifts, the gossip, and the partying. Animist Iban communities in particular are notorious party animals (unlike some of their Christian counterparts), and you'll be invited to join in the excessive rice-wine drinking, raucous dancing and forfeit games that last late into the night. Finally, exhausted, you hit the sack – either on a straw mat right there on the *ruai*, or in a guest lodge next door.

15 JOINING THE PARTY AT AN IBAN LONGHOUSE

One of the many great things about having a Thai massage is that there's no oil or lotions involved, so you don't need to strip off and there's none of that **embarrassing tussle with paper knickers**; you can also get your massage pretty much anywhere. This could be at a temple – in particular at **the famous Wat Pho in Bangkok**, historic centre of Thai massage therapy – at a hotel spa, or, most enticingly (and cheaply), on the beach. **A two-hour session under a palm tree will cost you no more than $10**, the soothing soundtrack of gently lapping waves will be genuine, and you should emerge feeling like you've had a good yoga workout, both relaxed and energized, but without having made any of the effort yourself.

16 Ironing out the kinks in Thailand

It can come as a shock the first time a Thai masseur uses his or her elbows on your back, then brings heels, feet and knees into play, pulling and pushing your limbs into contorted yogic stretches. But it's all carefully designed to exert a gentle pressure on your vital energy channels, and it's what distinguishes the Thai approach from most other massage styles, which are more concerned with tissue manipulation.

Thais will visit a masseur for conditions that might send others scuttling to the pharmacist – to alleviate fevers, colds and headaches, for example. But healthy bodies also benefit; it's said that regular massage sessions produce long-term well-being by stimulating the circulation and aiding natural detoxification. And it's certainly an idyllic way to while away a few languorous hours on the beach.

need to know

Bangkok's **Wat Pho** has been the leading school of Thai massage for hundreds of years, and masseurs who train there are considered the best in the country. Wat Pho also runs massage courses in English (ⓦwww.watpomassage.com; $175), as does the long-established **Old Medicine Hospital** in Chiang Mai (ⓦwww.thaimassageschool.ac.th; from $100).

17

The biggest Buddhist stupa in the world: Borobudur

O n one level, the Buddhist monument at Borobudur is just one huge stone comic strip: the life of the Buddha told in a series of intricate reliefs carved around a gigantic stupa-shaped structure rising from central Java's fertile plains. But it's also a colossal representation of the Buddhist cosmic mountain, Meru. Built sometime around the ninth century AD by the short-lived Saliendra dynasty, occupying some two hundred square metres of land and incorporating 1.6 million blocks of local volcanic rock, it is the largest monument in the southern hemisphere.

Much of Borobudur's appeal, however, comes not from its enormity but from the little details: the delicately sculpted reliefs, eroded down the generations but still identifiable and alive with warriors, maidens, the devout and the debauched, as well as elephants, turtles and other creatures. Beginning at ground level, pilgrims would walk clockwise around the monument, studying the frieze as they went, before moving up to the next level. Borobudur can be viewed as one enormous 34.5-metre-high educational tool; a complete circuit would take the pilgrims and monks, most of whom would have been illiterate, through the life of the Buddha. Starting from his earthly existence, represented by the friezes on the first four tiers, it ends with his attainment of Nirvana – or "nothingness" – at the tenth and top level, here represented by a large, empty stupa. The friezes on the first four "earthly" tiers are, on an artistic level, the most remarkable, but it is the upper five galleries that tend to linger in the memory, as the outside walls disappear, allowing you to savour the views over the lush Javanese plateau to the silent, brooding volcanoes beyond.

need to know: Borobudur (⊕www.borobudurpark.com; daily 6am–5.30pm; $10) is served by frequent buses from Yogyakarta, 40km southeast, and can be visited as a day-trip. An overnight stay, however, allows you both to watch the sun set over the monument in the evening and to visit early the next day before the crowds arrive.

18

Want to feel like a local on a weekend in Bangkok? Then you need to go shopping. Specifically, you need to go to Chatuchak Weekend Market and spend a day rifling through the eight thousand-plus stalls of what some claim to be the world's biggest market. It's certainly a contender for the world's sweatiest and most disorientating, with a quarter of a million bargain-hunters crammed into an enormous warren of alleyways, zones, sections and plazas. The maps and occasional signs do help, but much of the pleasure lies in getting lost and happening upon that unexpected must-have item: antique opium pipe, anyone?

Alongside the mounds of second-hand Levis and no-brand cosmetics you'd expect to find in Southeast Asia's most frantic flea market, there's also a mass of traditional handicrafts from Thailand's regions. Fine silk sarongs from the northeast, triangular cushions and mulberry-paper lamps from Chiang Mai, and hill-tribe jewellery and shoulder bags are all excellent buys here. But what makes Chatuchak such a shopaholic's dream is its burgeoning communty of young designers. Many of Asia's new fashion and interior design ideas surface here first, drawing professional trend-spotters from across the continent. The clothing zone is the obvious beacon, with its hundreds of mini-boutiques displaying radical-chic outfits and super-cute handbags, while the lifestyle zone brims over with tasteful ceramics and sumptuous furnishings.

Need a break from the achingly fashionable? Then wander through the pet section, perhaps lingering to watch Bangkokians' poodles getting their weekly beauty treatments, before enjoying a blast of natural beauty among the orchids and ornamental shrubs. And spare a thought for your stomach, for the market is full of foodstalls specializing in anything from barbecued chicken to coconut fritters. There's even a tiny jazz café for that all-important chillout between purchases. And don't let your feet call a premature end to the day: simply get yourself along to the foot-massage stall in Aisle 6, Zone B.

need to know: Chatuchak Weekend Market (Sat & Sun 7am–6pm) is in north Bangkok, near Mo Chit Skytrain and Kamphaeng Phet subway stations.

Braving the dragons' den on Komodo Island

Trekking through the dense undergrowth of Komodo Island, knowing all the while that the world's largest lizard could be lying in wait just a few inches from you, is one of Southeast Asia's most adrenaline-inducing activities.

Measuring up to three metres long, if you were to use just one word to describe the dragons it would be "revolting", given their scarred, leathery skin and a mouth that drips with viscous, bacteria-filled saliva. But they're also deadly, with a tail that could knock a buffalo off its feet and talons that are designed to scythe through tendons to cripple their prey.

The beasts' kingdom is a huddle of half a dozen Indonesian islands between Flores and Sumbawa, the two largest of which – Komodo and Rinca – together form the Komodo National Park. From the moment your boat pulls up on the island and you're met by a welcoming party of deer (who prefer to hang out on the beach rather than risk foraging amongst the dragons inland), it becomes clear that this is a world where nature, rather than man, still holds the upper hand; there's only one village on Komodo, and none at all on Rinca. So, when on a guided trek around Komodo's dry, scrunching forest, it's the local fauna you'll encounter: from deer to buffalo, horses to cockatoos, plus, of course, the dragons themselves, who spend their days lying motionless in the sun, tasting the air with their tongues in their quest for new prey. To stroll around their realm is unnerving but, like all encounters with unusual beasts, it's also exhilarating. And if you follow your guide's advice, you'll live to tell the tale too.

need to know: Most trips to Komodo National Park (ⓦwww. komodonationalpark.org) are organized from Labuanbajo on the island of Flores. Two-day tours cost from $40 per boat per day including food.

Exhilarating though the ridgetop views often are, it's not the scenery that draws travellers into the hills of northern Thailand, but the people who live in them. There are some **four thousand hill-tribe villages** in the uplands of Chiang Mai and Chiang Rai provinces, peopled by half a dozen main tribes whose ancestors wandered across from Burma and China. They have subsistence-farmed up here for two hundred years and continue to observe **age-old customs and beliefs**, making visiting them a fascinating, and popular, trip.

The trekking between villages is moderately taxing – you're in the hills after all – but the trails are well worn and a good guide will bring the landscape alive, pointing out **medicinal plants and elusive creatures** along the way. The highlights, though, are the villages themselves, clusters of **stilted bamboo huts** close by a river, invariably wreathed in wood-smoke and busy with free-ranging pigs and chickens. Village architecture varies a little between tribes, particularly where **animist shrines and totems** are concerned, for each group lives by distinct traditions and taboos. But the diverse costumes are more striking: the **jangling headdresses of the Akha women** decorated with baubles hammered out of old silver coins; the **intricately embroidered wide-legged trousers** worn by the Mien; the pom-poms and

The hills are alive

Day-Glo pinks and greens favoured by the Lisu. Many hill-tribeswomen make their living from weaving and embroidering these traditional textiles and buying direct is a good way of contributing to village funds.

need to know

Insensitive tourism has caused many problems in hill-tribe villages, and exploitation by travel companies is widespread, so choose your trekking company wisely. In Chiang Mai, both **Eagle House** (www.eaglehouse.com) and the **Trekking Collective** (www.trekkingcollective.com) are recommended operators. Near Chiang Rai, the **NGO Mirror Art Foundation** (www.hilltribetour.com) also leads culturally sensitive treks. Three-day treks cost from $60 per person.

trekking in **northern Thailand**

21 Island-hopping in the

If you thought Alex Garland's tropical-island classic *The Beach* was inspired by Thailand, think again; it was the Philippines, particularly the spectacular islands and lagoons of the Bacuit archipelago in Palawan, where tourists are still relatively thin on the ground but surely won't be for long. It's not hard to see why Garland was so bewitched by this place: 45 stunning limestone islands rise dramatically from an iridescent sea. Most have exquisite palm-fringed beaches, so you shouldn't have too much trouble finding your own piece of paradise for the day. All you need to do is pack yourself a picnic, hire yourself an outrigger boat – known locally as a *banca* – and ask the boatman to do the rest.

Start by chugging gently out to Miniloc Island, where a narrow opening in the fearsomely jagged karst cliffs leads to a hidden lagoon known as Big Lagoon, home to hawksbill turtles. A couple of minutes away, also at Miniloc, is the narrow entrance to Small Lagoon, which you have to swim through, emerging into a natural amphitheatre of gin-clear waters and the screech of long-tailed macaques.

Other islands you shouldn't miss? Well, take your pick. Pangalusian has a long stretch of quiet beach; Tres Marias has terrific snorkelling along a shallow coral reef; and Helicopter Island (named after its shape) has a number of secluded sandy coves where your only companions are monitor lizards and the occasional manta ray floating by.

The culmination of a perfect day's island-hopping should be a sunset trip to Snake Island, where you can sink a few cold San Miguels (take them with you in an ice box), and picnic on a slender, serpentine tongue of perfect white sand which disappears gently into shallow waters that are ideal for swimming.

need to know

There are daily flights from Manila to El Nido on the Palawan mainland, departure point for the archipelago, with SEAIR and Islands Transvoyager Incorporated. A number of exclusive resorts have been established on some of the islands, or there's plenty of budget accommodation in rustic El Nido itself.

Bacuit
archipelago

the Philippines

22 Balinese theatrics in Indonesia

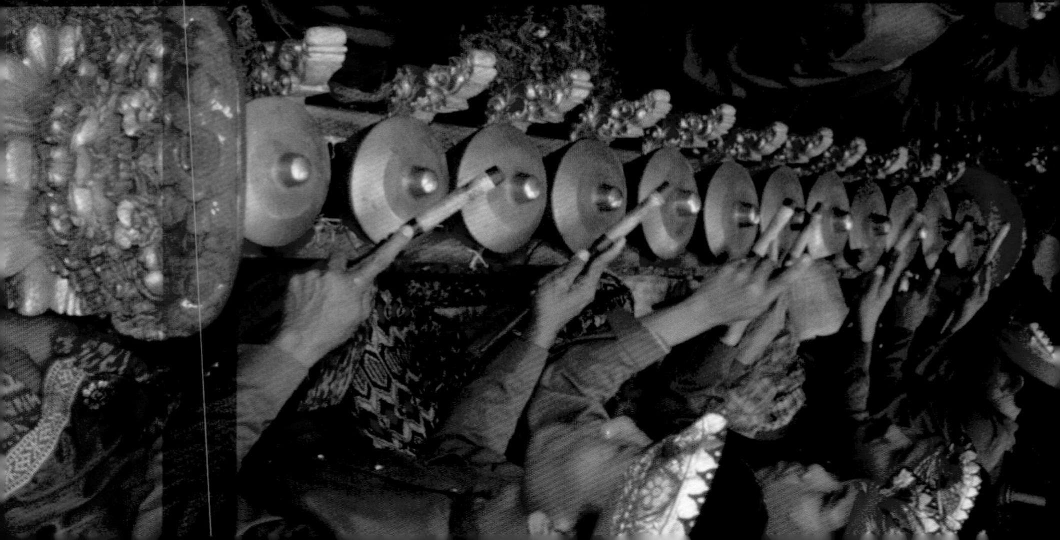

On the island of Bali, a Hindu enclave in the majority Muslim nation of Indonesia, the gods and spirits need regular appeasing and entertaining, and on special occasions there is ritual music and dancing. Temple festivals are so frequent here that you've a good chance of coming across one, but there are also **dance performances staged for tourists** at the palace in Ubud, the island's cultural hub. Even though the programme has been specially tailored, there is nothing inauthentic about the finesse of the palace performers. And the setting – a **starlit courtyard** framed by stone-carved statues and an elaborate gateway – is magnificent.

Every performance begins with a priest sanctifying the space with a sprinkle of holy water. Then **the gamelan orchestra strikes up**: seated cross-legged either side of the stage, the twenty-five musicians are dressed in formal outfits of Nehru jacket, traditional headcloth and sarong. The light catches the bronze of their **gongs, cymbals and metallophones**, the lead drummer raises his hand, and they're off, racing boisterously through the first piece, producing an **extraordinary syncopated clashing of metal on metal**, punctuated by dramatic stops and starts.

Enter the dancers. Five sinuous barefooted young women open with a ritualistic welcome dance, scattering flower petals as an offering to the gods. Next, the poised refinement of the Legong, performed by three young **girls wrapped in luminous pink, green and gold brocade**, the drama played out with gracefully angled hands, fluttering arms and wide flashing eyes. Finally it's the **masked Barong–Rangda drama**, the all-important pitting of good against evil, with the loveable, **lion-like Barong** stalked and harassed by the powerful **widow-witch Rangda, all fangs and fingernails**. With typical Balinese pragmatism, neither good nor evil is victorious, but, crucially, spiritual harmony will have been restored on the Island of the Gods.

need to know

Dance performances are staged nightly at Ubud Palace; tickets cost $5. Ubud is about 30km from Bali's international airport; it's easily reached by bus and is full of charming hotels and guest houses.

Everyone over thirty in Cambodia has lived through the genocidal Khmer Rouge era. The woman who runs your guest house in downtown Phnom Penh; the moto driver who tried to rip you off on the ride down from the Thai border; your Angkor temples tour guide; your waiter at the seaside café in Sihanoukville. At the Tuol Sleng Genocide Museum you'll learn something of what that means.

A former school on the outskirts of Phnom Penh, Tuol Sleng, code-named S-21, was used by the Khmer Rouge to interrogate perceived enemies of their demented Marxist-Leninist regime. During the Khmer Rouge rule, from 1975 to 1979, some fourteen thousand Cambodians were tortured and killed here, often for the crime of being educated: for being a teacher, a monk, or a member of the elite; for wearing glasses; for being a discredited cadre. We know this because the Khmer Rouge were meticulous in their documentation. When the Vietnamese army arrived at S-21 in January 1979 they found thousands of mugshots of former prisoners, each of them numbered, along with reams of typed "confessions".

Those black and white photographs fill the downstairs walls of the museum today. There are rows and rows of them: men, women, children, even babies. Only seven prisoners survived S-21; one of them, Ung Pech, became the museum's first director. When the museum opened to the public in 1980, thousands of Cambodians came here to look for evidence of missing relatives.

The interior of the prison has in part been left almost as it was found. Tiled floors, classrooms crudely partitioned into tiny cells, shackles, iron bedsteads and meshed balconies. Elsewhere, graphic paintings by another survivor, Vann Nath, depict the torture methods used to extract confessions; some of these confessions are also reproduced here. Once they'd been coerced into admitting guilt, prisoners were taken to the Choeung Ek Killing Fields and murdered. Choeung Ek, 12km southwest, is now the site of another memorial. Distressing as it may be, unless you see these important places for yourself no trip to Cambodia is complete.

need to know
The Tuol Sleng Genocide Museum (daily 7.30–11.30am & 2–5pm; $2) is off Street 13 on the southern fringes of Phnom Penh.

23 Visiting the
Tuol Sleng
Genocide Museum,
Cambodia

24 Volcanic activity: sunrise on Mount Bromo

It's not the most famous, the most active or the biggest volcano in the world, but Indonesia's 2392-metre-high Mount Bromo is one of the world's most picturesque – in a dusty, post-apocalyptic sort of way. The still-smoking and apparently perfectly symmetrical cone rises precipitously out of a vast, windswept, sandy plain. This is the Sea of Sand, actually the floor of an ancient crater (or caldera), stretching up to ten kilometres in diameter and with walls some three hundred metres high.

Though the locals will try to persuade you to take their horse, it's an easy enough walk to the summit, with no climbing ability required. Setting off an hour before sunrise, you follow a path across the Sea of Sand to the foot of Bromo's vertiginous cone. A small matter of 249 concrete steps up past crowds of others with the same idea – it's one of Java's most popular attractions – leads to the crater rim and a view down onto the fumaroles belching noxious sulphuric fumes. But the rewards of climbing Bromo are not olfactory, but visual: for if the gods of climate and cloud-cover are on your side, a flamboyant golden sunrise awaits, casting its orange glow over the vast emptiness of the sandy basin, with Java's lush green landscape stretching to the horizon beyond.

need to know
Mount Bromo is the main attraction of East Java's Bromo-Tengger-Semeru National Park. Most people stay in the nearby village of Cemoro Lawang, a two-hour bus drive from Probolinggo on Java's north coast. It's possible to climb Bromo year-round, though if it's raining or particularly cloudy you might prefer to stay in bed and wait until the next day.

25

Feeling fruity in the Mekong Delta, Vietnam

need to know

My Tho is a ninety-minute bus ride from Ho Chi Minh City. One-day delta tours cost from $20 per boat. Home-stays cost $15 per person and can be arranged at local tourist offices or as part of a cycling tour through Sinhbalo Adventure Travel in Ho Chi Minh City (@www.cyclingvietnam.net).

If you're looking for a classic Southeast Asian scene, Vietnam's Mekong Delta, south of Ho Chi Minh City, will do the trick. This is an area of vivid green rice paddies, conical-hatted farmers and lumbering water buffaloes; of floating markets and villages built on stilts. Lush orchards overflow with mangoes, papayas and dragonfruit; plantations brim with bananas, coconuts and pineapples. And through it all wind the nine tributaries of the Mekong River, their canals and tributaries nourishing this fruitbasket of Vietnam, busy with sampans, canoes and houseboats. It is the end of the run for Asia's mighty Mekong, whose waters rise over four thousand kilometres away in the snows of the Tibetan plateau and empty out here, into the alluvial-rich plains fringing the South China Sea.

For the fifteen million people who live in these wetlands, everything revolves around the waterways, so to glimpse something of their life you need to join them on the river. Boat tours from the market town of My Tho will take you to nearby orchard-islands, crisscrossed by narrow palm-shaded canals and famous for their juicy yellow-fleshed sapodilla fruits. At Vinh Long, home-stay programmes give you the opportunity to sample the garden produce for dinner and spend the night on stilts over the water. Chances are your host-family catch fish as well – right under their floorboards in specially designed bamboo cages, so the daily feed is simply a matter of lifting up a plank or two. Next stop should be Can Tho, the delta's principal city, to make the ride out to the enormous floating market at Phung Hiep. Here at the confluence of seven major waterways, hundreds of sampans bump and jostle early each morning to trade everything from sugar cane to pigs – and of course fruit.

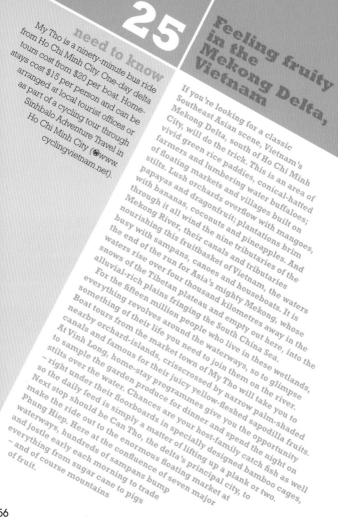

Ultimate
experiences
Southeast
Asia
miscellany

1 Food

▶▶ Chillis

Many Southeast Asian cuisines make liberal use of the chilli, which can come as quite a shock to the uninitiated palate. The fire is concentrated in the seeds and flesh around them; the smaller chillies are often the hottest. On the international Scoville scale of chilli hotness, a normal green bell pepper rates zero units, a mid-sized Thai chilli comes in at 45,000 units, a tiny "mouse-shit" Thai chilli clocks up 80,000 units, and a Mexican habanero tops out at 300,000.

▶▶ Five of the best foods to try

Amok dt'ray in Cambodia. Fish curry made with a rich coconut sauce and baked in banana leaves.

Làp in Laos. A salad of raw minced meat spiced up with garlic, chill and fish sauce.

Lechon in the Philippines. Roast pig stuffed with pandanus leaves.

Nem in Vietnam. Fresh spring rolls stuffed with herbs, crabmeat, rice vermicelli and beansprouts.

Tom yam kung in Thailand. Fragrantly spiced hot and sour prawn soup.

2 Populations

Brunei 372,000	**Cambodia** 12 million	**Vietnam** 83 million
East Timor 925,000	**Malaysia** 23 million	**The Philippines** 87 million
Singapore 2.7 million	**Burma** 47 million	
Laos 6 million	**Thailand** 63 million	**Indonesia** 200 million

3 Five fabulous hotels

Amandari, Bali, Indonesia. Tastefully understated villa compounds overlooking Ubud's lush Ayung River valley.

Swissôtel The Stamford, Singapore. The second tallest hotel in the world offers stunning views and classy rooms.

The Datai, Langkawi, Malaysia. Harmonious retreat that's surrounded by rainforest but beside the beach.

Grand Hotel D'Angkor, Siem Reap, Cambodia. Historic, colonial-era opulence close by the Angkor ruins.

The Tongsai Bay, Ko Samui, Thailand. Set in beautiful grounds fronting a private beach.

4 Stinking fruit and foul flowers

The **rafflesia** is the world's largest flower. Found in the rainforests of Indonesia, Malaysia and Thailand, its blooms measure up to 90cm across and can weigh as much as 11kg. It flowers during the rainy season and is almost as famous for its horrible stink (similar to rotting meat) as for its size.

The **durian** is Southeast Asia's most prized (and expensive) fruit, but it smells so bad – somewhere between detergent and dogshit – that many airlines and hotels ban people from consuming it on their premises. Nor does everyone appreciate the taste, which aficionados liken to mature cheese mixed with caramel; many will spend up to $100 on a good one.

"Like eating a magnificent raspberry blancmange in a foul public toilet."

Novelist Anthony Burgess on the durian experience

5 Sport

At the Olympics, Southeast Asian countries usually do best at **badminton**. Indonesia's badminton players won three medals at Athens in 2004, one gold and two bronze, putting them in third place behind China and Korea.

In Thailand, **muay thai** (Thai boxing) enjoys a following similar to football in Europe. Every province has a stadium and the biggest bouts are broadcast every Sunday afternoon on TV, watched by large noisy crowds in noodle shops around the country.

Basketball is the national sport of the Philippines, with twelve teams competing in the major league, the Philippine Basketball Association, and hundreds of neighbourhood games happening on barrio courts across the nation.

6 Festivals

What	When	Where
Ati-Atihan Mardi Gras-style extravaganza	mid-Jan	Kalibo, the Philippines
Thaipusam Hindu festival of ritual body piercing	Full moon, Jan or Feb	Singapore and Kuala Lumpur, Malaysia
Chinese New Year Dragon and lion dances, Chinese opera, fireworks and food stalls	Jan or Feb	Chinatowns across Southeast Asia, but especially in Singapore and peninsular Malaysia
Sumba Pasola Fierce battles between hundreds of spectacularly costumed horsemen, held to restore cosmological balance	Feb or March	Sumba, Indonesia
Buddhist New Year National water fights to symbolize mass spiritual cleansing	mid-April	Cambodia, Laos and Thailand
Tet Doan Ngo Traditional dragon boat races and parades mark the summer solstice	May or June	Vietnam
Gawai Dayak All-night drinking and party games in the longhouses to celebrate the end of the rice harvest	June	Sarawak, East Malaysia
Loy Krathong Palm-leaf baskets full of flowers and candles are floated on rivers and shorelines to honour the water goddess	Full moon, Oct or Nov	Thailand

7 The Mighty Mekong

The Mekong is one of the great rivers of the world, the twelfth longest on the planet. From its source 4920m up on the east Tibetan Plateau it roars down through China's Yunnan province, then snakes its way a little more peaceably through Laos, by way of the so-called Golden Triangle, where Burma, Thailand and Laos touch. From Laos it crosses Cambodia and continues south to Vietnam, where it splinters into the many arms of the Mekong Delta before flowing into the South China Sea, 4184km from where its journey began.

8 Architecture

Until 2003, the **Petronas Towers** in Kuala Lumpur were the tallest buildings in the world (452m). The 88-storied tapering twin towers are joined by a sky-bridge at the forty-second floor, which is as high as visitors are allowed. The towers played a starring role in the 1999 action movie *Entrapment*, alongside Sean Connery and Catherine Zeta Jones.

"It makes you laugh with delight to think that anything so fantastic could exist on this sombre earth. They are gorgeous; they glitter with gold and whitewash, yet are not garish."

Somerset Maugham enjoys the temples of Bangkok

When designing a **traditional house** on the Indonesian island of Bali, the architect begins by noting down the vital statistics of the head of the household. The house-compound's walls, for example, must be the sum of a multiple of the distance between the tips of the householder's middle fingers when the arms are outstretched, plus the distance from his or her elbow to the tip of their middle finger, plus the width of their fist with the thumb stretched out. The different structures of the compound are believed to reflect the human body: the family shrine is the head, the main pavilions are the arms, the courtyard is the navel, the kitchen and rice barn are the legs and feet, and the garbage tip is the anus.

9 Java Man

Excavations in 1891 and 1936 near Solo on the Indonesian island of Java revealed the **oldest hominids** then discovered, dating back about seven hundred thousand years. These relics of *Homo erectus* were dubbed Java Man, but later lost the title of oldest hominid to Nariokotome Boy, whose 1.6 million-year-old remains were found in Kenya's Great Rift Valley.

10 Religion

Country	Predominant faiths
Brunei	Islam
Cambodia	Theravada Buddhism
East Timor	Roman Catholicism
Indonesia	Islam; with animist, Christian and Hindu minorities
Laos	Theravada Buddhism
Malaysia	Islam; with Buddhist, Hindu and Christian minorities
The Philippines	Roman Catholicism
Singapore	Mahayana Buddhism; with Muslim, Hindu, Sikh and Christian minorities
Thailand	Theravada Buddhism
Vietnam	Mahayana Buddhism

Buddhist monks are forbidden to have any close contact with women, which means, if you are female, that you mustn't sit or stand next to a monk (even on a bus), brush against his robes, or hand objects directly to him. When giving something to a monk, the object should be placed on a nearby table or passed to a layman who will then hand it to the monk.

Indonesia is the largest Islamic nation in the world. The most orthodox region of the country is in North Sumatra, where Islamic preachers first arrived from India in the eighth century; elsewhere, local Islamic practices often display animist, Buddhist and Hindu influences. Most of Indonesia's many tribal communities are animists, especially in West Papua, Sumatra and Kalimantan. Though their beliefs and customs vary widely, animists share the view that nearly everything in the world has a spirit, in particular trees, plants, rocks and rivers. On the island of Bali, the predominant faith is a blend of Hinduism and animism.

▶▶ Five important religious sites

Omar Ali Saifuddien mosque, Bandar Seri Begawan, Brunei. The magnificently opulent focal point of the Bruneian capital.

Wat Phra Kaeo, Bangkok, Thailand. Dazzlingly ornate temple that houses the most sacred image in the country, the tiny Emerald Buddha.

Angkor Wat, Cambodia. Iconic twelfth-century Hindu temple complex, with later Buddhist additions, featuring exquisite bas-reliefs.

San Agustin Church, Manila, the Philippines. Sixteenth-century stone church with an exceptional Baroque interior that miraculously survived World War II intact.

Borobudur, central Java, Indonesia. The biggest Buddhist stupa in the world, built in the ninth century with stone friezes that tell the Buddha's life story.

11 Five memorable train rides

The Jungle Railway, Malaysia. A 14-hour ride through mountainous jungle between Gemas and Kota Bharu.

The Death Railway, Thailand. An amazing feat of engineering with a tragic history, built by World War II PoWs along the scenic River Kwai valley.

Eastern and Oriental Express, Thailand, Malaysia and Singapore. Elegant, wood-panelled carriages, a panoramic viewing car and cordon-bleu meals makes this the most luxurious – and expensive – way to travel the 52 hours between Bangkok and Singapore.

Reunification Express, Vietnam. Chug gently down the length of Vietnam, from Hanoi in the north to Ho Chi Minh City in the south, in around 34 hours.

Phnom Penh to Battambang, Cambodia. Cambodia's only train runs just once a week, takes up to 15 hours to cover the 290-kilometre journey, and is predictably basic: many passengers bring their own hammocks.

12 Etiquette

In Buddhist, Islamic and Hindu cultures, the **head** is considered the most sacred part of the body and the **feet** the most unclean. This means that it's very rude to touch another person's head or to point your feet either at a human being or at a sacred image. Be careful not to step over any part of a person who is sitting or lying on the floor without first offering an apology. Shoes are nearly always taken off before going inside a home or place of worship.

13 Getting around

Cycle rickshaws in Cambodia, Vietnam, Thailand and Indonesia. Sedate, human-powered, private transport around town.

Jeepneys in the Philippines. American World War II jeeps converted into idiosyncratically decorated buses.

Longtail boats in Thailand. Elegant but noisy wooden boats steered with an elongated propeller shaft and used for island-hopping and river travel.

Motorbike taxis almost everywhere. Perfect for getting through the jams in grid-locked cities and essential out in the sticks.

Tuk tuks in Thailand. Iconic open-sided three-wheelers powered by deafeningly loud two-stroke engines.

14 Literature

▶▶ Southeast Asian travel

Playing with Water by James Hamilton Patterson. Lyrical account of time spent living alone on an uninhabited island in the Philippines.

Into the Heart of Borneo by Redmond O Hanlon. Amusing tale of an expedition into the Sarawak jungle in search of the two-horned rhinoceros.

The River's Tale by Edward A Gargan. A year-long odyssey from the source of the Mekong in Tibet to its delta in Vietnam.

Ring of Fire by Lawrence and Lorne Blair. Classic, beautifully photographed account of a decade of wanderings around the Indonesian archipelago.

Ant Egg Soup: The Adventures of a Food Tourist in Laos by Natacha Du Pont De Bie. A foodie's funny, original tour of Laos and its cuisine.

▶▶ Southeast Asia in literature

The Sorrow of War by Bao Ninh. Modern classic about a very young North Vietnamese army captain.

All That is Gone by Pramoedya Ananta Toer. Short stories set in east Java by the late, politically outspoken, Pramoedya Ananta Toer, Indonesia's most famous writer.

The Quiet American by Graham Greene. Prescient novel about American meddling in Vietnam, set in the 1950s.

The Beach by Alex Garland. Cult thriller that uses a Thai setting to explore travellers' self-defeating quest for undiscovered utopias.

Dogeaters by Jessica Tarahata Hagedom. Gritty contemporary novel set in Marcos-era Manila and peopled by a cast of underworld characters.

The epic Hindu poem the **Ramayana**, written in India in the fourth century BC, has inspired countless sculptures, paintings, dance performances and shadow-puppet dramas across Southeast Asia and still provides moral and practical lessons. It dramatizes the eternal conflict between good and evil: Rama, an avatar of the Hindu god Vishnu, represents the forces of good, and the demon king Ravana is his evil nemesis.

15 Colonialism and independence

Thailand is the only Southeast Asian country never to have been colonized by a European nation. Historically, the major Western players in the region have been: France, in Laos, Cambodia and Vietnam; Britain, in Burma, Malaysia and Singapore; and the Netherlands, in Indonesia.

Timor Leste (East Timor) became the world's newest nation on May 20, 2002, having finally won autonomy from Indonesia. It had previously been under Portuguese rule for four centuries until Indonesia invaded the territory in 1975.

In 1898, America fought Spain for control of the **Philippines** and won. The Philippines finally gained independence on July 4, 1946.

"If the Tiger does not stop fighting the Elephant, the Elephant will die of exhaustion."

Ho Chi Minh anticipates Vietnam's victory over the US

16 Natural phenomena

Indonesia is the world's largest archipelago, comprising 17,508 islands, of which about 6000 are inhabited. The Philippines comes in second, with 7107 islands, forty percent of them inhabited. Both are among the most volcanically active regions in the world, being within the highly volatile **Pacific Ring of Fire**. More than half the world's active volcanoes are in the Ring and over 80 percent of the world's earthquakes occur along it.

However the **Sumatra–Andaman earthquake** of December 26, 2004, which triggered tsunamis across the region, was within the Alpide belt. It registered between 9.1 and 9.3 on the Richter scale, lasted longer than any other earthquake recorded and created the longest rupture in the Earth's seabed ever observed. Indonesia was the worst affected country with over 130,000 people losing their lives.

17 Shopping

▶▶ Five things to take home

Batik sarongs and shirts from Malaysia and Indonesia.

Silk Lustrous sheens and beautiful designs in Thailand, Laos, Vietnam and Cambodia.

Woodcarvings from Indonesia. Kalimantan and West Papua produce unusual tribal carvings, Bali makes contemporary figurines.

Triangular pillows from Thailand. Buy one with attached cushions to use on a chaise longue or as a spare bed.

Conical hat The trademark Vietnamese all-weather headgear.

18 Traditional therapies

In Laos, it's common to go for a **herbal sauna** before having a traditional massage. The herbs in question include tamarind, carambola, lemongrass and eucalyptus, though exact recipes are closely guarded.

The most famous traditional beauty treatment in Indonesia is the exfoliation rub, **mandi lulur**, which is based on a paste made from turmeric. Javanese brides are said to have a *lulur* treatment every day for the forty days before their wedding ceremonies.

19 Trade

As the main thoroughfare between the Indian Ocean and the Pacific Ocean, the **Straits of Malacca**, which separates the Indonesian island of Sumatra from peninsular Malaysia, is one of the most important shipping lanes in the world. It's Southeast Asia's Suez Canal, transporting over twenty percent of the world's maritime trade. This includes a quarter of all seaborne oil shipments, as it's the shortest route between the Persian Gulf and Asian markets. It's also extremely narrow, at less than three kilometres wide near Singapore and just 25 metres deep at its shallowest point.

20 Performing arts

Southeast Asia has some unique performing art forms; five of the best are:

Water-puppet theatre in Hanoi, Vietnam. Charming folk-tales performed by puppets that literally dance on the water.

Wayang kulit shadow puppet dramas in Malaysia and Indonesia. Stick puppets act out epic tales and contemporary satire from behind a torchlit screen.

Kecak dance in Bali, Indonesia. Spectacular drama starring an a cappella "monkey" chorus of fifty chattering, bare-chested men.

Apsara dance in Cambodia. Elegant courtly dance that evokes ancient Hindu goddesses.

Gamelan performances in Indonesia. Classical dance accompanied by the shimmering sounds of brass xylophones and gongs.

21 Political leaders

Thailand is a constitutional monarchy and King Bhumibol is the world's longest-serving head of state, having celebrated his 60th year on the throne in 2006.

The **Lao People's Democratic Republic** is a one-party dictatorship and one of the world's last official Communist states. It's run by the Lao People's Revolutionary Party, which has traditionally followed a Marxist–Leninist ideology but now looks increasingly to China.

"The contemptible Pot was a lovely child."

Loth Suong, older brother of Pol Pot

22 Languages

Bahasa Malay and its near-identical offshoot **Bahasa Indonesia** (which was only invented in the 1950s, as a unifying language for the newly independent Indonesian nation) are among the easiest languages to master. They are written in Roman script, have no tones and use a straightforward grammar. Verbs have no tenses and nouns take no articles, with plurals simply a question of saying the word twice: thus "car" is *mobil*, and "cars" *mobil-mobil*, sometimes written *mobil2*.

"Unity in diversity"

The national motto of Indonesia, whose people speak more than 350 local languages

The **Tai family** of languages includes Thai; Lao; Shan (Tai Yai), spoken in Burma; Phuan, spoken in Laos and parts of Thailand; and Tai Leu spoken by the Dai minority of China's Yunnan province. All are tonal languages, making them difficult for Westerners to master. Thai has five tones – low, middle, high, falling and rising – by which the meaning of a single syllable can be altered in five different ways. For example, using four of the five tones you can make a sentence from just one syllable: "*mái mài mâi mǎi*" which means "New wood burns, doesn't it?".

Bangkok's official Thai name has 64 syllables, which makes it the longest place name in the world. In translation it means something like "Great city of angels, the supreme repository of divine jewels, the great land unconquerable, the grand and prominent realm, the royal and delightful capital city full of nine noble gems, the highest royal dwelling and grand palace, the divine shelter and living place of the reincarnated spirits".

23 Southeast Asian reefs

Southeast Asia hosts over thirty percent of the world's coral reefs, the vast majority of which are in Indonesian and Philippine waters. These nations' reefs are the most biodiverse marine habitats on the planet, supporting 2500 different species of fish, countless molluscs and crustaceans, and 600 varieties of reef-building coral.

▶▶ **Top five dives**

Pulau Sipadan, Sabah, Malaysia. Shore and cave diving, barracuda, white-tip sharks and masses of turtles.

Tubbataha Reef, Palawan, the Philippines. Giant manta rays, tuna, dolphins, black-tip reef sharks and even whale sharks.

Puerto Galera, Mindoro, the Philippines. So rich in marine life, it's UNESCO-listed.

Similan Islands, Thailand. Manta rays, barracuda, giant lobster, reef sharks, white-tips, morays and turtles.

Alor, Nusa Tenggara, Indonesia. Dog-tooth and skipjack tuna, sharks, turtles, rays, dolphins – and whales.

24 Economics

The average per capita income in **Singapore** is around US$28,000. In **Laos** it's US$300.

Vietnam has the second fastest-growing economy in the Asia-Pacific region, after China. In 2006, just 12 years after the US lifted their trade embargo against their old enemy, Vietnam was accepted into the World Trade Organization as its 150th member nation.

"We would not have made economic progress if we had not intervened on very personal matters – who your neighbour is, how you live, the noise you make, how you spit, or what language you use."

Lee Kuan Yew, prime minister of Singapore from 1959 to 1990, on his authoritarian style of government

25 Southeast Asia on film

Apocalypse Now (Francis Ford Coppola, 1979). Operatic, psychedelic take on the insanity of the American War in Vietnam.

Iron Ladies (Youngyooth Thongkonthun, 2000). The enjoyably camp true-life dramas of a successful Thai volleyball team made up of transsexuals and transvestites.

The Killing Fields (Roland Joffé, 1984). Harrowing dramatization of a Cambodian journalist's life under Pol Pot's tyrannical regime.

Manila in the Claws of Neon (Lino Brocka, 1975). Classic noir depiction of a bewildered innocent's journey to the Philippine capital in search of his beloved.

Cyclo (Tran Anh Hung, 1995). Shockingly graphic thriller, dubbed the Vietnamese *Pulp Fiction*, about a cycle-rickshaw driver's increasingly desperate life in Ho Chi Minh City.

Ultimate
experiences
Southeast
Asia
small print

25

ROUGH GUIDES – don't just travel

We hope you've been inspired by the experiences in this book. To us, they sum up what makes Southeast Asia such an extraordinary and stimulating place to travel. There are 24 other books in the 25 Ultimate Experiences series, each conceived to whet your appetite for travel and for everything the world has to offer. As well as covering the globe, the 25s series also includes books on **Journeys, World Food, Adventure Travel, Places to Stay, Ethical Travel, Wildlife Adventures** and **Wonders of the World**.

When you start planning your trip, Rough Guides' new-look guides, maps and phrasebooks are the ultimate companions. For 25 years we've been refining what makes a good guidebook and we now include more colour photos and more information – on average 50% more pages – than any of our competitors. Just look for the sky-blue spines.

Rough Guides don't just travel – we also believe in getting the most out of life without a passport. Since the publication of the bestselling Rough Guides to **The Internet** and **World Music**, we've brought out a wide range of lively and authoritative guides on everything from **Climate Change** to **Hip-Hop**, from **MySpace** to **Film Noir** and from **The Brain** to **The Rolling Stones**.

Publishing information

Rough Guide 25 Ultimate experiences Southeast Asia Published May 2007 by Rough Guides Ltd, 80 Strand, London WC2R 0RL
345 Hudson St, 4th Floor, New York, NY 10014, USA
14 Local Shopping Centre, Panchsheel Park, New Delhi 110017, India
Distributed by the Penguin Group
Penguin Books Ltd,
80 Strand, London WC2R 0RL
Penguin Group (USA)
375 Hudson Street, NY 10014, USA
Penguin Group (Australia)
250 Camberwell Road, Camberwell, Victoria 3124, Australia
Penguin Books Canada Ltd,
10 Alcorn Avenue, Toronto, Ontario, Canada M4V 1E4
Penguin Group (NZ)
67 Apollo Drive, Mairangi Bay, Auckland 1310, New Zealand

Printed in China
© Rough Guides 2007

80pp
A catalogue record for this book is available from the British Library
ISBN: 978-1-84353-827-1

The publishers and authors have done their best to ensure the accuracy and currency of all the information in **Rough Guide 25 Ultimate experiences Southeast Asia**, however, they can accept no responsibility for any loss, injury, or inconvenience sustained by any traveller as a result of information or advice contained in the guide.

1   3   5   7   9   8   6   4   2

Rough Guide credits

Editors: Claire Saunders, Alice Park
Design & picture research: Link Hall, Jj Luck
Cartography: Maxine Repath, Katie Lloyd-Jones

Cover design: Diana Jarvis, Chloë Roberts
Production: Aimee Hampson
Proofreader: Edward Aves

The authors

Lucy Ridout (Experiences 1, 3, 4, 5, 6, 7, 9, 11, 12, 14, 15, 16, 18, 20, 22, 23, 25, Miscellany) is co-author of Rough Guides to Thailand, Bangkok, Thailand's Beaches and Islands, Bali and Lombok and First-Time Asia.

David Dalton (Experiences 2, 8, 10, 21) is author of The Rough Guide to the Philippines.
Henry Stedman (Experiences 13, 17, 19, 24) is co-author of The Rough Guide to Indonesia.

Picture credits

Fly Less – Stay Longer!

Rough Guides believes in the good that travel does, but we are deeply aware of the impact of fuel emissions on climate change. We recommend taking fewer trips and staying for longer. If you can avoid travelling by air, please use an alternative, especially for journeys of under 1000km/600miles. And always offset your travel at www.roughguides.com/climatechange.

ROUGH GUIDES

New Zealand
Budapest
Thailand
Greece
Punk
Italy
India

Over 70 reference books and hundreds of travel
guides, maps & phrasebooks that cover the world

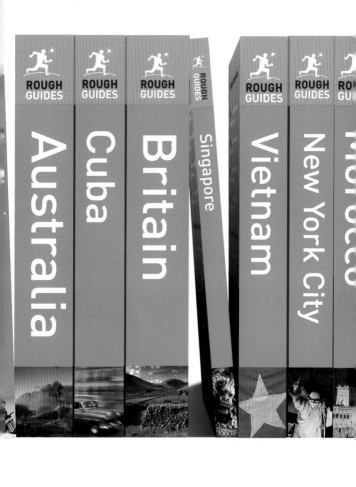

Index

a

Angkor 8
architecture 63
Ati-Atihan festival 10

b

Bacuit archipelago 48
Bali 50
Bangkok 42
Banaue 22
beaches 14, 48
Bromo, Mount 54
boat trips 12, 16, 34,
48, 54
Borobudur 40

c

Cambodia 8, 52
Chatuchak market 42
Chiang Mai 46
Chiang Rai 46
cooking 28

d

diving 26, 71
durian 61

e

earthquakes 68
eating 28, 60
etiquette 66

f

festivals 10, 62
film 72
food 28, 60

h

Ha Long Bay 16
Hoi An 24
hotels 60

i

Indonesia .. 32, 40, 44, 50, 54
islands 14, 16, 34, 44, 48

j

Java 40, 54
Java Man 64

k

Kalibo 10
Kinabalu, Mount 30
Komodo dragons 44

l

language 70
Laos 12, 18
literature 66
longhouses 36
Louang Phabang 18

m

Malaysia 20, 30, 36
massage 38
Mekong river 12, 56, 63
music 50, 69

o

orang-utans 32

p

performing arts 69

r

rafflesia 61
rainforests 20
reefs 26, 70
religion 64
rice terraces 22

s

Sarawak 36
Siem Reap 8
shopping 42, 68
sport 61
Sumatra 32

t

Taman Negara 20
temples 8, 18, 40, 65
Thailand 14, 28, 34,
38, 42, 46
transport 65, 66
trekking 22, 30, 46, 54
tsunami 68
Tubbataha Reef 26
Tuol Sleng Genocide
Museum 52

v

Vietnam 16, 24, 56

w

wildlife 20, 26, 32, 44

Phang Nga, etc.

Phang Nga 34
Philippines 10, 26, 48
Phnom Penh 52
politics 67, 69